ALDO ICE CREAM

Aldo starts his ninth summer with modest ambitions: learning to swim and sampling each of the thirty flavors available in the local ice-cream store. But when Mrs. Sossi asks him to help her deliver Meals On Wheels to the elderly and housebound, Aldo becomes unexpectedly busy. Finding ways to fill his new friends' empty days challenges his ingenuity, but the real challenge comes when Aldo decides to buy his sister the ice-cream freezer she wants for her birthday.

"Aldo's suburban middle-class family provides a gentle, easygoing setting where Hurwitz's narrative talents shine."

—School Library Journal

Aldo Ice Cream

JOHANNA HURWITZ

ILLUSTRATED BY JOHN WALLNER

Harcourt

Orlando   Boston   Dallas   Chicago   San Diego

Visit *The Learning Site!*
www.harcourtschool.com

This edition is published by special arrangement with
Puffin Books, a division of Penguin Putnam Inc.

Grateful acknowlegment is made to Puffin Books,
a division of Penguin Putnam Inc. for permission to reprint
Aldo Ice Cream by Johanna Hurwitz, illustrated by John Wallner,
cover illustration by Karen Schmidt.
Text and illustrations copyright © 1981 by Johanna Hurwitz;
cover illustration copyright © 1989 by Karen Schmidt.

Printed in the United States of America

ISBN 0-15-314351-7

3 4 5 6 7 8 9 10   060   02 01 00

In memory of
Mabel Zahn,
children's librarian,
New York Public Library.

Contents

Aldo Ice Cream

1

Meals-on-Wheels

Aldo Sossi lay flat on his stomach with his chin resting in the dirt. He was very, very still.

"You look as though you're dead," said his sister Elaine, as she stepped over his motionless body.

Aldo wasn't dead. He was feeling fine. In fact, he had never felt better. Summer vacation had come, and he hoped it would last forever. There were a hundred things he wanted to do.

Earlier this morning he had gone to his first swimming lesson at the local pool. At first he had been nervous. He was certain that he would be the only nine-year-old boy in all of Woodside, New Jersey, who didn't know how to swim. But, to his relief, there were other children in the group who were his age. He hoped that by the end of the summer he could swim. So far he had learned to put his head underwater and to open his eyes.

"Bye," Aldo called to Elaine and his other big sister, Karen, who were going off to their advanced swimming lesson. Aldo concentrated on the ground again. He was observing the ants that were walking about. The ants were very tiny, and unless you looked closely you couldn't see them at all. Aldo watched how they circled some bread crumbs that he had dropped. He knew that in a few minutes they would lift the crumbs and carry them to their home, even though the small bits of bread were much larger than they were.

Ants were very interesting, thought Aldo. He was fascinated by bugs and animals of all sorts. Sometimes, when his sisters teased him, Aldo thought he liked animals even better than people. His most favorite animals were his two cats, Peabody and Poughkeepsie, who were sleeping in the sun in front of the house.

Aldo sometimes wondered what it would feel like to be a cat. He thought having a long tail that he could move at will would be fun. And he liked to imagine taking big jumps and landing easily on four paws. But this morning, during the swimming lesson, Aldo had started thinking for the first time how much fun it would be if he were a fish. If he were a fish living in the river or in the ocean, he could explore the shells, plants, and other fish deep below.

Even being an ant seemed fun to Aldo. He watched how they disappeared right in front of his eyes only to reappear a moment later. Imagine being so small that you could get through the tiniest of cracks. An ant could explore anywhere! Aldo sighed. Too bad he couldn't change into an ant for just a little while to see what it felt like.

"Aldo! Aldo, where are you?" a voice called out. Mrs. Sossi was looking for her son. "I have a job for you. I need some help with the Meals-on-Wheels, and both Elaine and Karen are off at their swimming class."

Aldo stood up and brushed the dirt off his jeans. "Will I get paid?" he asked eagerly. He had been hoping to find a way to make some money.

"No. Meals-on-Wheels is volunteer work."

"You mean you work for free?" asked Aldo. "I thought grown-ups always got paid when they worked."

"How about when I do your laundry or cook supper?" asked Mrs. Sossi. "That's work, but I don't get paid."

"That's different," said Aldo. "We're your family, and you love us."

16

"Yes," agreed his mother, looking at Aldo's dirty jeans. "But I don't love your laundry. I don't get any money for my volunteer work, but I get paid with the satisfaction of knowing that I'm helping the elderly and sick people. I bring food to some who are unable to prepare their own meals. It needs to be done, and even if these people aren't my relatives, I want to help them."

Aldo was disappointed about the money, but he was still curious and so he went with his mother quite willingly. At the local hospital, they were given four covered trays of hot food and paper bags containing sandwiches and small containers of milk. There were several other volunteers who were also picking up food to be delivered. They all had their own route to follow.

Aldo looked at the list of names and addresses that his mother placed beside her on the front seat of the car. "Don't any of these old people have relatives to take care of them?"

"No. The people on my list are alone all the time. Perhaps they have family that lives far away, or perhaps they have no family. But they still want to live in their own home, and they can, at least for the moment, if someone brings them food each day."

"It seems so sad," said Aldo. "When you and Dad get old, I'll stay nearby and help take care of you." He thought of the ants in the backyard. At this very moment they were carrying crumbs to one another.

"Well, that's nice," said Mrs. Sossi, taking one hand off the steering wheel for a moment and patting her son's shoulder. "But we don't have to worry about that now."

Their first stop was at the home of an elderly man.

"Hello, Mr. Puccini," said Mrs. Sossi. "This is my son, Aldo, and he's helping me today."

Mr. Puccini nodded his head, but he didn't say anything. He was hardly taller than Aldo, and his hair was pure white. Mrs. Sossi removed the hot food from the tray. Aldo saw that there were two slices of lamb, a baked potato, green peas, and a salad. In a separate little dish was rice pudding with a tiny dab of whipped cream.

"Aldo, take out a container of milk and a paper bag," instructed Mrs. Sossi, pointing to a plastic shopping bag that Aldo had carried into Mr. Puccini's house for her.

When all the food was set out, Mrs. Sossi said good-bye to Mr. Puccini. "Have a good day,"

she told him. "I'll see you again next week."
Mr. Puccini nodded his head. He hadn't said
a single word.

"Why didn't we stay longer?" asked Aldo,
as they got back into the car. "He seemed so
lonely, and we didn't even give him a chance
to talk."

"I know." Mrs. Sossi sighed. "He has rarely
spoken in all these weeks that I've been delivering food. That is why this is such an important service. At least each person gets a
small bit of human contact along with his food.
But we have to hurry, or the meals for the
other people will get cold."

The car pulled up in front of a small apartment building. "Now you will meet Mrs.
Allenwood," said Aldo's mother.

Mrs. Allenwood was exactly the opposite of
Mr. Puccini. She was tall and very healthy
looking, but her arm was broken and in a sling,
so she wasn't able to cook for herself. And unlike Mr. Puccini, she spoke a great deal.

"I'm from the school that says youngsters should help," she said approvingly, when Mrs. Sossi introduced her to Aldo. She looked eagerly at the food as Aldo and his mother removed it from the tray. "Ah, good! A potato! I'm from the school that says you should have a potato every day, and yesterday they gave me noodles instead," she complained.

"Be careful," Mrs. Sossi cautioned Mrs. Allenwood, as the older woman picked up her milk container and rushed to put it into the refrigerator. "You don't want to have another fall."

"I'm from the school that says it's important to keep active. I'm not going to sit around like an invalid," said Mrs. Allenwood.

"Well, have a good day," said Mrs. Sossi, "and enjoy your potato."

Aldo and his mother went out of the apartment. As they got back into the car, Aldo said, "Mrs. Allenwood sure went to a lot of schools."

"It's just an expression," said Mrs. Sossi.

They drove on to two other homes. In each one there lived someone who could not shop or prepare her own food. Mrs. Nardo was recovering from a heart attack, and Mrs. Thomas had arthritis.

When all the deliveries had been made, Aldo and his mother returned the empty trays and the plastic shopping bag to the hospital. "Tomorrow someone else will do the job," said Mrs. Sossi. "But I'll need you again next Thursday, when it's my turn."

"Sure," said Aldo. "It's very interesting to meet all those people. But I wish we could do something else to cheer them up. They all look so sad and lonely. It must be very boring to stay home alone all day long." Aldo thought for a moment. "I liked Mr. Puccini. He has a nice face. I wish he would speak to me sometime."

"Here," said Mrs. Sossi, digging into her coin purse. "This afternoon you can treat DeDe to an ice cream." DeDe was Aldo's best friend. "It will be payment for your help this morning."

For a moment Aldo was torn. If his mother didn't get paid, he really shouldn't accept money. On the other hand, she might have given him the money even if he hadn't helped her deliver the meals. "Thanks," said Aldo, taking the dollar bill that she held out to him. "I'm from the school that loves ice cream."

After lunch, DeDe came over with her dog, Cookie. One of the plans that they had made for the summer was to see how many tricks they could teach Cookie. Already the dog had learned to shake paws. However, Aldo had pointed out to DeDe that she always gave her left paw. "You're supposed to shake with your right," he said.

"I never noticed," DeDe admitted. "Cookie must be left-pawed."

Aldo told DeDe all about the Meals-on-Wheels. "Those were really old people I saw this morning," he said. "I thought my grandparents were old, but Mrs. Thomas is old enough to be the mother of my grandmother. And she hardly has any teeth," he added, remembering the old woman he had met. Aldo showed DeDe the dollar that he had received from his mother. "Let's go for the ice cream right now," he suggested.

A new ice-cream store had recently opened in Woodside. It sold thirty different flavors, and another of Aldo's plans was to sample every single one before the summer was over. There were certainly enough days ahead of him. The only problem was, where would he get enough money?

"What flavor are you going to choose?" Aldo asked DeDe, as they walked along the street together. "Will you try something new?"

"Chocolate," said DeDe. "I always get chocolate."

"Maybe you'll find something that's even better," suggested Aldo.

"I know I like chocolate," explained DeDe. "So what's the point of trying something I might like better when I might not like it as much?"

That didn't make much sense to Aldo, who loved to try new things. However, he was a vegetarian, which meant that he never ate meat. And since DeDe didn't make fun of him for *his* eating habits, he felt he had to respect her feelings about ice cream. She was a *chocolatarian,* he decided. As for Aldo, he would skip the old flavors like chocolate and vanilla and concentrate on new ones like pistachio mint and blueberry cream.

It was hard to make a decision as he read down the printed list. Last week the whole Sossi family had walked over to the ice-cream store, and Aldo had an almond-buttercrunch cone. It had been delicious, and he would have loved another one now. But if he repeated flavors, he would never get to try them all.

DeDe was already licking her chocolate

cone. Cookie whined softly, and DeDe lowered the cone so the dog could have a lick.

"Come on, slowpoke," DeDe said to Aldo.

"Peach ripple!" said Aldo, making an instant decision.

As he took the first cool, sweet lick he thought of something. "Imagine we were animals like fish or ants," he said to DeDe. "We would never eat ice cream. It's good that we're human beings.

"Yep!" said DeDe, biting into her cone. "But don't forget about Cookie. She likes ice cream."

Aldo bent down and gave the dog her lick. "Here, Cookie," he said. "This is your chance to try a new flavor."

Unlike her owner, the dog seemed very willing to experiment with something new.

"She likes it!" said Aldo, as he savored licks of the peach-ripple cone. "Ice cream is my favorite food," he said.

"Maybe I should call you Aldo Ice Cream

instead of Applesauce," said DeDe, referring to his nickname at school.

"Don't you dare," said Aldo, but he wasn't angry. "I wonder what flavor I should get next time?" he asked.

It was going to be a good summer.

Job Hunting

By the end of the second week of July, Aldo could do the dead man's float, and Cookie could roll over and play dead.

Despite these two somber-sounding activities, life at the Sossi house was very lively. Elaine had begun the summer with a series of baby-sitting jobs. Although she was only fourteen and a half she appeared to be the richest member of the family. She was always counting her money. Sometimes she made more than five dollars in a single afternoon or evening. Aldo's sister Karen was feeling bad.

"I wish someone would ask me to baby-sit for them," she said, one night at dinnertime. "After all, I'm practically thirteen, and that's just as grown-up as fourteen," she insisted. "I need money too."

"Cheer up," said Mr. Sossi. "If I've been able to support you this long, I can manage a few more months or even years."

"Really?" said Karen, brightening.

"Of course!" Her father said.

"Well, there's something I want very much," said Karen. "Actually, everyone in the family would get pleasure out of it."

"What is it?" asked her mother.

"I saw a machine for making ice cream in the hardware store. Wouldn't it be super if we could make our own ice cream? We could even invent our own flavors."

"Oh, let's get one," said Aldo. He knew that Karen enjoyed cooking, and even though she sometimes overcooked or burned some of her recipes, he didn't see how she could spoil ice cream.

"How much does it cost?" asked Mrs. Sossi.

"Only forty-nine dollars and ninety-five cents," said Karen.

"*Only!*" said both Mr. and Mrs. Sossi at the same time.

"I'm afraid that's too extravagant a wish, Karen," said Mr. Sossi.

Just then the phone rang. Aldo jumped up from the dinner table to answer it. "It's probably for Elaine," said Karen gloomily, and she was right.

"Soon Elaine will need a secretary to handle all her calls," commented Mr. Sossi, helping himself to another piece of fish.

They could all hear Elaine speaking on the phone. "Oh, I'm sorry," she said. "I'm already baby-sitting this coming Saturday night."

"Tell her about me," shouted Karen, jumping up from the table.

"Why don't you call my friend Sandy?" suggested Elaine, ignoring Karen, who was standing right beside her. "Her number is 612-9065."

"You're mean," Karen accused her sister, when she got off the phone. "Why didn't you tell her about me? I could have sat."

"I had to give Sandy's number," said Elaine, defending herself. "She's my best friend!"

"Well, Karen is your best sister," offered Aldo.

"Karen is my *only* sister," said Elaine. "But I have many friends, and Sandy is the best one. Besides, she has given my name to a lot of people. That's how I got started sitting in the first place."

"I don't care," said Karen. "I hate you."

"Then I certainly won't ever give your name to anyone," said Elaine.

"Girls, stop this bickering at once," interrupted Mrs. Sossi. "There are loyalties to family and loyalties to friends. And besides, I promise you, Karen, that before you know it you will have more requests for baby-sitting than you can possibly handle. You just have to be patient a little bit longer."

Aldo felt sorry for Karen. He wished there were some way that he could help her find a job. It would be wonderful if she could earn enough money to buy the ice-cream freezer. Then they could make all their own ice cream, and he wouldn't have to buy it in town.

After supper he got the idea of studying all the classified advertisements in the *Penny-saver*, which was a little local paper that was delivered free of charge to the door each week. It was always filled with ads of used furniture for sale or people who would clean out roof gutters. Mr. Sossi studied it each week in hopes of finding a used Ping-Pong table. And Mrs. Sossi often went to garage sales that she read about. Mr. Sossi called them "garbage sales," but nevertheless his wife had already bought a rug for Karen's room and a pair of wicker lawn chairs as a result of reading the little paper. Maybe there is a job for Karen, Aldo thought. He read every advertisement carefully to find something that would be just right for her. Aldo turned page after page. There was nothing. Suddenly his eye stopped at an ad that sounded perfect for himself. It read:

Great baby-sitting job. 9-year-old boy. 3 to 5:30 Monday through Friday, some evenings. Call after 6 P.M. #423-0798.

Aldo rushed to the telephone. Elaine was talking to Sandy. It was silly how much they spoke on the phone when Sandy lived just down the street. Elaine could practically have a conversation with Sandy by sticking her head out the window. Aldo gestured to Elaine that he wanted to make a phone call.

"Make like a tree and leave," she said, turning her back on him.

Aldo waited a few minutes. He was worried

that someone else would call and get the job ahead of him. He went back to the telephone. Elaine was still talking. She looked at Aldo and said, "Pretend you're a drum and beat it."

"Very funny," said Aldo, but he didn't think her remark was funny at all.

The third time Aldo approached her, Elaine said, "Make like a bee and buzz off."

By now Aldo was so angry at Elaine that instead of walking away again, he stood by the phone going "Bzzzzzzzz. Bzzzzzzzz."

"Aldo, leave me alone," said Elaine.

"Bzzzzzzzz. Bzzzzzzzz," was all that he answered.

"*Les petits frères,*" Elaine complained in French to Sandy. "I hate little brothers."

From the way she spoke, you would think she had six little brothers and not just one, Aldo thought, getting angrier than ever. "Bzzzzzzzzzz," he repeated.

"What's all this noise?" asked Mr. Sossi,

walking past the phone. "Elaine, are you still talking? Get off at once. You've been on the phone for over an hour."

"I've got to get off," said Elaine. "I'll see you tomorrow morning, Sandy. *Au revoir.*" Finally she hung up.

Clutching the newspaper in his hand, Aldo dialed the number. He hadn't told anyone in his family about the job. He wanted to surprise them with the fact that someone was advertising for a nine-year-old boy. It made him feel really grown-up. Unfortunately, the voice on the other end of the phone explained that they were looking for a baby-sitter for their nine-year-old son and they didn't want another nine-year-old boy. Aldo hung up, his face burning with embarrassment. There was no job for him. He didn't need a baby-sitter, and he couldn't imagine why that other, unknown nine-year-old boy did either.

Aldo went out into the backyard, where his parents were sitting, reading. "Mom, can you think of a way for me to earn some money?" he asked.

"What's this money mania around here?" asked Mr. Sossi. "First your sisters, and now you. Money is necessary in this world, but I don't think you have to start worrying about it at age nine."

"I'm not worrying," said Aldo, "but I'd like to buy that ice-cream freezer for Karen's birthday."

"Aldo, that's a lovely thought, but you'll never be able to get forty-nine dollars and ninety-five cents by her birthday on September first," his mother said.

"I've got almost all summer left. I'm going to try," said Aldo with determination.

"Well, it's certainly better than the last time Aldo was asking about money," said Mrs. Sossi to her husband. "Remember last year when he wanted to buy an ant farm? Ugh!"

"That was when we lived in the city," Aldo reminded her. "I don't need an ant farm now that we have a backyard full of our very own ants."

"Just don't bring any of them visiting inside the house," said Mrs. Sossi. "It's quite a job to get rid of them."

The Quarter-a-day Plan

Even if he didn't receive money, Aldo considered his weekly chore of helping his mother with the Meals-on-Wheels a job. He was proud to be able to carry the trays of food, and he liked visiting with the elderly people. But one thing kept bothering him. "Mr. Puccini never says a single word," he told DeDe. "Sometimes Mrs. Thomas or Mrs. Nardo only say hello and good-bye, but at least they say something. Mr. Puccini has never said anything at all."

41

It was the third Thursday in July and they were sitting in the Sossi car, on the way to deliver the food. DeDe was being fitted for braces this summer, and most Thursdays she had to go to the dentist. But she had specially changed her appointment so she could accompany Aldo and his mother.

"Maybe he'll say something today," said DeDe.

Mrs. Sossi parked the car in front of Mr. Puccini's house, and the three of them got out. She rang the doorbell. After a minute the little man opened the door.

"Hi, Mr. Puccini," said Aldo.

The old man nodded his head, but he didn't say anything. "This is my friend DeDe. She's helping us today," said Aldo.

They went into the kitchen and unloaded the food onto the table. There was sliced turkey with cranberry sauce, rice, carrots, and a small salad. There was also a dish of chocolate pudding. As they set the little plastic dishes on the table, Aldo smiled to himself. He could already imagine Mrs. Allenwood complaining, "I'm from the school that says you should have a potato."

"Enjoy your food, Mr. Puccini," said Mrs. Sossi. "We'll see you next week." The old man nodded his head. Aldo wondered if he could speak. Perhaps there was something wrong with his throat or his voice. As they walked through the small hallway leading to the door, Aldo noticed the door to the living room was open. Usually it was closed. Aldo looked through the door and saw an enormous fish tank near the window.

"Oh, Mr. Puccini, could I look at your fish?" he asked.

Again the old man nodded his head, but for the first time there was a trace of a smile on his face.

There was not one but three tanks side by side, and they contained fish of many varieties. There were also interesting plants and there were snails climbing up the sides of the tanks.

"What are those?" asked Aldo, pointing to

some tiny fish with bright stripes. "They look as if they had electric lights inside them."

"That's why they're called neon fish," said Mr. Puccini.

"I wish I could have some fish too," said Aldo. "But we have two cats, and my father says they would try to knock over the tank and catch the fish."

"These fish are more interesting than a tele-

vision show," said Mr. Puccini, breaking his silence a second time. "I watch them for hours and they keep me company."

"Aldo, we'd better get moving," said Mrs. Sossi. "The other meals will get cold."

"Good-bye, Mr. Puccini," said Aldo. "Can I look at the fish again next week?"

"Sure," he answered. "They're not going anyplace. They'll be here waiting for you." Mr. Puccini smiled at Aldo. "It's nice to meet someone who is interested in them too."

"Well," said DeDe, when they got back in the car. "You sure made him talk."

"He seemed so pleased that you were interested in his fish," said Aldo's mother.

"Yes," agreed Aldo. "I'm glad he has something to keep him company. I wouldn't be lonely with those tanks of fish."

When they got to Mrs. Allenwood's, DeDe learned about the schools she came from. That day Mrs. Allenwood said, "I'm from the school that says a dry July means a wet August," and

"I'm from the school that says waste not, want not." And as Aldo had anticipated, she complained about the rice. "I'm from the school that says you should have a potato every day," she reminded them.

The children found it hard to keep from giggling at her comments.

The other stops were quite routine. They greeted the recipients of the meals and emptied the trays onto their kitchen or dining-room tables. The job was finished quickly, and they drove first to the hospital to deposit the empty trays for use the next day and then on to the Sossi's house.

After a lunch of cheese sandwiches and chocolate milk, during which Aldo said, "I'm from the school that says you should have lunch every afternoon," and DeDe said, "I'm from the school that says you should have supper every evening," Aldo asked, "Mom, can I borrow a quarter from you?"

He had discussed his wish to save enough

money to buy the ice-cream freezer for Karen with DeDe. She didn't know how he could earn money, but she had told him that once her father had explained that if you saved just a quarter a day, every day for a year, at the end of the year you would have ninety-one dollars. Aldo didn't have enough fingers to figure that one out, but he had sat down with a pencil and paper and added twenty-five and twenty-five and twenty-five and twenty-five and twenty-five over and over again. The figures added up to a lot of money, and saving ninety-one dollars didn't seem as if it would be so hard to do. Especially since he had begun with a dollar in his bank, which was equal to four days of saving.

But in the past few days he had discovered that meeting his quota of a quarter a day was much harder than he had expected. After the first four days were over, he had borrowed a quarter from his father. The next day he borrowed a quarter from Karen. Yesterday, after much coaxing and promises not to bother her when she was on the telephone, Elaine had grudgingly lent him a quarter too. Now it was his mother's turn.

"Mom, can I borrow a quarter from you?" Aldo asked again.

"I'll tell you what," suggested Mrs. Sossi. "I'll give you a grocery list. If you and DeDe walk over to the supermarket for me, I'll let you keep the change. It should be even more than a quarter."

There were just a few items on Mrs. Sossi's grocery list: half a gallon of milk, a can of salmon, a bunch of bananas, a bottle of ketchup, and a loaf of bread. She gave Aldo a five-dollar bill. "You should get almost a dollar back," she said. "You can put it into your ice-cream-freezer account."

But when the cashier rang up the total at the supermarket, the amount came to five dollars and seven cents. "All I have is five dollars," said Aldo, embarrassed to be caught with less than he needed.

"Wait," said DeDe. She dug into the pocket of her jeans and pulled out a dime. "My mother always makes me carry ten cents in case I have to phone her."

So they paid for the groceries and walked home. Aldo was very dejected. "How could so few things cost so much money?" he asked.

"My mother says there is an awfully big inflation these days. Every time she goes shopping things cost more than they did the last time. Probably all the prices went up since the last time your mother bought them," she explained.

Mrs. Sossi said exactly that. "It must be inflation!" She handed DeDe a dime, and in exchange DeDe gave her the three cents change that she had gotten in the supermarket.

"I'm sorry, Aldo," said Mrs. Sossi, giving her son the three pennies. "This is all I have for you today."

"Three pennies?" said Aldo. "What can I do with three pennies?"

He wondered if Elaine would lend him another quarter. Perhaps he should just return the quarters that everyone had lent him and abandon the quarter-a-day plan. If only he could think of another way to get some money.

Cats-on-Wheels

By the last week of July, Aldo could do the dog paddle and Cookie would sometimes fetch a ball or a stick that was thrown to her. Now apparently Cookie would have a vacation from learning tricks, because DeDe was going away for three weeks to stay with her grandparents in Michigan. She was going to fly on a plane by herself, and they would meet her at the airport.

"I'll write you a letter," DeDe promised,

51

"and when I come home, we'll still have time to teach Cookie some more tricks before school opens."

"I wonder if I could teach Peabody and Poughkeepsie some tricks while you're away," said Aldo. However, the cats were not agreeable to this plan. Karen said that cats were not as smart as dogs, but Mr. Sossi reminded Aldo that the cats were more than ten years old, and in cat time that was equivalent to seventy years.

"You wouldn't expect to teach a seventy-year-old man new tricks, so don't expect it of the cats," said Mr. Sossi.

"Well, Aldo certainly taught Mr. Puccini how to be friendlier," said Mrs. Sossi. "He never used to speak at all, and these days we are hardly in the door before he is telling Aldo all about his fish and how they are doing."

Mr. Puccini and Aldo certainly had become very good friends. And twice, even when-it wasn't their day to deliver meals, Aldo had pedaled over to Mr. Puccini's house on his bicycle to visit with the old man and his fish. Mr. Puccini knew a great deal about ichthyology, which is the study of fish. He could talk and talk about the little creatures in his tanks, and Aldo the animal lover enjoyed listening to him. Mr. Puccini seemed a different man from the silent, nodding person that Aldo had met on his first trip delivering Meals-on-Wheels. Aldo learned that Mr. Puccini was much older than Peabody and Poughkeepsie. He was eighty-three years old.

"How old were you when you started having fish?" Aldo asked Mr. Puccini.

"I was a young man," said Mr. Puccini. "I was only seventy-five then. I was passing by a pet shop one day, and I saw a tank of fish in the window. I watched them for a bit, and then I bought one goldfish and a small glass bowl." He smiled at the three tanks of fish that he now owned. "After a couple of days I decided that my fish looked lonely. So I went back and bought a second one. Then the two fish looked crowded in the little bowl, and so I bought a tank. Then I thought that I should have some plants and more fish. Before I knew it, I had all this."

On one of his visits, Mr. Puccini asked Aldo if he would be able to buy some fish food. Aldo was glad to help, and so on his next call he brought Mr. Puccini some fish-food-on-wheels too. The little can contained oat flour, shrimp meal, fish liver, squid, fish roe, kelp, mosquito larvae, brine shrimps, aquatic plants, agar-agar, chlorophyll, and carotene. But when Aldo sprinkled some into the aquariums, the food looked like bits of colored paper. It didn't look very appetizing, and Aldo was glad that the food they brought to Mr. Puccini was more appealing.

Although Mr. Puccini was Aldo's favorite person on the Thursday morning route, he was also interested in the others. He worried about the small, uninteresting supper of a sandwich and a piece of fruit that was left for them in a paper bag. And he also worried that they might be lonely and bored. At least Mr. Puccini had his fish for company and Mrs. Allenwood could take walks about the neighborhood. The others were restricted by their poor health to staying home all day long. There was a limit to how much television a person would want to watch. Everything gets boring after a while.

Mrs. Nardo told Aldo that she used to own a cat. It had died during the winter at the age of fourteen (which Aldo figured to be the equivalent of a human age of ninety-eight). "I'm too old to get a new cat," she said sadly. "My son says that I might trip over it, since my sight isn't so good. I know he's right. My sister, who lives in Pennsylvania, tripped over her dog and broke her hip."

Aldo got an idea. "Could we bring our cats with us next time in the car when we deliver the food?" he asked his mother. "Since Mrs. Nardo can't have a cat of her own, Peabody and Poughkeepsie could come for a visit. It would cheer her up."

"Absolutely not," said Mrs. Sossi. "That's all I need—two cats jumping on the trays of food! Do you realize what a mess they would make of everything? Besides, Mrs. Nardo is still recovering from her heart attack. She doesn't need strange cats in her house."

Aldo wasn't convinced. Peabody and Poughkeepsie weren't *strange* cats. Anyhow, one of the advantages of living in Woodside was that he could get on his bike and go most anywhere he wanted in the town. He would take the cats and visit with Mrs. Nardo on his own. Maybe they would stop and visit with Mrs. Thomas too.

Aldo didn't mention his plan to his mother, but that very afternoon, while she was off shopping, he went into the basement and found an empty carton. He also located a piece of heavy string. Then he had to go hunting for the cats. Peabody was sunning himself on the front step, but Poughkeepsie was nowhere in sight. After fifteen minutes of searching the possible cat hiding places, Aldo gave up. He would take Peabody for a visit today, and next time it would be Poughkeepsie's turn.

Aldo picked the cat up and put him into the carton. Cats love cartons, and if Peabody had found one lying on the ground, he would have quickly entered and explored it. But being put into a carton was a different matter entirely. With great effort, Aldo managed to keep Peabody from jumping out of the carton while he tied it shut with the string. Aldo balanced the box on the handlebars of his bicycle and started off. From inside the box the cat began to meow loudly.

"I'm not kidnapping you, Peabody," said Aldo, as he pedaled along. "I'm just taking you for a visit." The cat moved about inside

the box, and it wobbled violently on the
handlebars. With great difficulty Aldo managed to keep his balance and to keep on going.
Carrying Peabody was much harder than he
had expected, and he thought it was a good
thing after all that he had brought only one
cat with him.

When he reached Mrs. Nardo's house, he
jumped off his bike and carried the carton to
her front door. He rang the bell.

"Why, Aldo," said Mrs. Nardo, when she opened the door. "Is that a box full of food?"

"It's better than food," said Aldo proudly, as he untied the knot in the string. "I brought my cat Peabody to visit with you." As he spoke the carton burst open and Peabody jumped out. He didn't wait to be introduced. Instead, he ran into the living room and hid under the sofa.

"He's not usually shy," Aldo apologized. "He'll probably come out in a minute."

"Well, let's sit down and wait for him," said Mrs. Nardo.

Aldo sat on the living-room rug and put his hand under the sofa. Mrs. Nardo sat in a big chair nearby.

"I never had a cat come and visit me before," she said. Then she corrected herself: "Well, I've had some stray cats walk through my yard. But I never had a cat come into my living room for an afternoon call."

They sat together. Aldo kept making the little sounds that he called the cats with at home. Mrs. Nardo's clock ticked loudly. Otherwise, all was still. Aldo was embarrassed by Peabody's behavior. This wasn't the way he had imagined the afternoon at all.

"I'm glad to see you, even if I can't see your cat," said Mrs. Nardo, smiling.

"I know how we could get him out," said Aldo, after all attempts to lure the reluctant visitor had failed. "Do you have a can of something that we could open. It could be anything. He always comes running when he hears the can opener at home."

Aldo and Mrs. Nardo went into the kitchen. She opened her cupboard. She removed a can of tomato sauce and a can of peaches. "I'll open this," said Mrs. Nardo, selecting the fruit.

Sure enough, even though he was in strange surroundings, the familiar sound of the can opener brought Peabody out from under the sofa.

"Too bad cats don't like peaches," said Mrs. Nardo. "I don't have anything to offer him." Then she remembered her supper bag, which Aldo had delivered that morning. She took it out of the refrigerator and opened the sandwich. It was roast beef. She removed the meat and broke it into little pieces in her fingers. Peabody watched with interest as she put the pieces on a saucer.

Aldo and Mrs. Nardo shared the peaches while Peabody ate the meat. "What will you eat tonight?" asked Aldo suddenly, as he spooned up the syrup from his fruit. "Peabody finished your supper."

"I can always boil an egg," said Mrs. Nardo. "Don't worry about me." She smiled at Aldo. "Wait till I tell my son that I had a gentleman caller and a cat for tea. Life is full of surprises."

She seemed so pleased that Aldo felt much better as he caught Peabody and put him back in the carton. Even if the visit wasn't exactly the way he planned it, the efforts of the afternoon were worthwhile after all. The carton

wobbled twice as much going home as coming. But again Aldo managed to keep his balance. He was exhausted from the new service that he had begun: animals-on-wheels.

When Mrs. Sossi saw Aldo pushing his bike with his wobbly carton up the driveway, she was very angry. "I told you not to take the cats visiting," she scolded. "You could have fallen off the bike and been hit by a car. Don't you ever try that again."

Peabody hissed at Aldo from inside the box. It was his way of saying that despite the roast-beef snack, he didn't approve either.

Hurricane Elaine

Mrs. Allenwood was right. She had said that a dry July meant a wet August. August began with rain. It poured every day for a week, and there were strong winds that broke many tree branches. The newspapers and television proclaimed that the bad weather was tropical storm Donald. Apparently it had been preceded by Annabelle, Brendon, and Clarice. These storms had gone out to sea.

"I have never seen so much rain," complained Mrs. Sossi.

"It never rained this much when we lived in New York," moaned Elaine.

"The weather in New York and the weather in New Jersey is virtually the same," Mr. Sossi assured his family. "If we have rain, they have rain."

"It's good for the farmers," said Aldo. "At least that's what they said on the news." It might have been good for the farmers, but the Sossi vegetable plot looked like a gigantic mud puddle, and many of the vegetables had fallen off their vines prematurely.

"I hate this weather," Elaine complained. She was to hate it even more the following day.

On the eighth of August, the newsboy threw the daily paper from his sack, and it landed smack in a puddle. Aldo always liked to get a quick look at the comics, but this time as he opened the soggy newspaper, he noticed first a large headline: *Watch Out for Hurricane Elaine.*

He shouted at the top of his voice, "Elaine! Elaine, come quick."

Elaine rarely did anything quickly, but the urgency in Aldo's voice brought her running. "What's the matter?" she asked.

"Look," said Aldo, handing her the newspaper. "Aren't you proud?"

Elaine read the headline. "Oh, no," she moaned. "More rain, and they're naming it after me. I refuse to take the blame."

"Well, it was going to rain anyhow," said Aldo. "I think it's nice to call the hurricane Elaine. Now your name is in the newspaper and you're famous."

"It does seem unfair," agreed Mrs. Sossi, who had come over to read the news and tried to console Elaine.

"They could have called it Elsa or Eunice or Evelyn or lots of other names," said Karen, who had joined them too. "But I think it's nice that it was named Elaine. I hope when they get to K they name the storm after me."

"I hope we never get to K," said Mrs. Sossi with a shudder. "By that time we'll have to build an ark. There's an inch of water in the basement already. And I've run out of old newspapers to soak it up."

"I could try to get some more," offered Aldo. "I could ask people if they have extra."

"It will be like having a reverse paper route," said Mrs. Sossi, laughing.

So Aldo took his mother's old shopping cart, which she had used for carting groceries when they lived in New York, and went off to see if he could get some newspapers. Karen went along to help him. Mrs. Sossi decided to stock up on some grocery items and get some candles too. "Sometimes the power lines come down during these big storms," she told the children.

The newspaper said that the storm was expected to arrive in their area around five in the afternoon. So they had plenty of time. Elaine and her mother brought seven large bags of groceries from the supermarket. In addition to things like eggs and bread, they had selected other things that Elaine felt were necessary for weathering a storm. There were four kinds of cookies and a large bag of potato chips.

Aldo and Karen returned with a collection

of newspapers from people with dry basements. They unloaded the cart and helped put the groceries away.

Mr. Sossi arrived home from work early. "We closed the office and sent everyone home," he explained. "We didn't want anyone driving during the storm. They are predicting winds up to seventy or eighty miles an hour."

Aldo found it hard to imagine that there would be such high winds as there was only a slight breeze at five o'clock. Mr. Sossi insisted that the weather could change from one minute to the next. Aldo brought Poughkeepsie and Peabody inside. They had been enjoying the fresh air after so many days of staying inside during the rain.

Mrs. Sossi turned on the radio for news of the storm, but there was nothing. Elaine turned on the television and saw the end of an old Humphrey Bogart movie while she waited for the six o'clock news. Mr. Sossi went upstairs to try a different station on the radio by his bed. Aldo sat looking out the window and watching for Hurricane Elaine.

At six o'clock there was still no sign of the storm. Mrs. Sossi suddenly remembered dinner and rushed into the kitchen to prepare something. They had been so busy thinking about the storm that they had all forgotten about eating.

"I'm worried about that old maple tree in the yard," said Mr. Sossi. "It has some dead branches, and we should have had them trimmed before now. The winds may knock them down, and they could damage the roof or break a window during the storm."

"We could put tape over the windows," suggested Mrs. Sossi. So they went hunting for the tape and put large strips of it across all the windows. Now if the glass broke, at least it wouldn't shatter.

"It's so quiet outside," said Karen. "I don't think we will get a storm at all."

71

"Hurricane Elaine isn't going to rain," chanted Aldo.

"Yes, I am," said Elaine. "I mean, yes, it is. Give it time." Now that she had gotten used to the idea, she almost liked having a hurricane with her name.

"This is what is meant by the calm before a storm," said Mrs. Sossi.

The family sat around watching a silly game show on the television. There didn't seem to be anything else to do. "I really should be cutting the grass," said Mr. Sossi. "But I don't want to begin and be interrupted in the middle."

"Could we open the potato chips?" asked Aldo.

"We're saving them to eat during the storm," Elaine reminded him. "And the cookies too," she added, knowing how her brother's mind and stomach worked.

"It sounds as if we're waiting for a movie to begin," said Mr. Sossi, switching off the television. "There must be something we can do as a family."

"We could play charades," suggested Mrs. Sossi.

"That's silly," said Elaine. "This isn't a birthday party."

Mrs. Sossi got up and started putting candles in every candle holder that she had. "I just remembered that I forgot to buy batteries for the flashlights. Soon it will be getting dark, so I had better be ready to light the candles if we need them."

"I could ride to town on my bike and get some batteries," offered Aldo.

"No. Stay right here," said his mother. "No one is leaving this house when a storm is approaching."

"I know something we haven't done in a long time," suggested Karen. "We could all play Monopoly together."

"That's so boring," said Elaine.

"Oh, yes, let's," cried Aldo.

Karen ran to her room and found the old Monopoly set. "I haven't played with this in years," she said.

"That's because it's so boring," said Elaine.

They sat on the living-room floor and set out all the pieces. Karen was the banker and distributed the money to the players.

"This is boring," said Elaine. She got up and brought the bag of potato chips to make the game more interesting. Aldo was going to say, "I thought we were saving them for the storm," but he wanted some too, so he kept his mouth closed, except to put chips into it.

"This is so boring," Elaine said again, when the bag of chips was empty. She went to the kitchen and returned with a box of cookies.

Everyone else was having fun. Monopoly was a silly game. But it was fun to have all that money to spend, even if it was fake. Aldo looked at the hundred-dollar bills in his hand. If only one of them were real, he thought. He could buy Karen the ice-cream freezer and

have enough left over to buy presents for everyone else he knew too. He had abandoned the quarter-a-day plan. It was much too hard to get the money every day.

"This is so boring," said Elaine. Aldo noticed that she said so whenever it wasn't her turn. When it was her turn, she concentrated quite hard on buying the best properties and making shrewd deals.

"I'm thirsty," he said.

Elaine was off in a flash and returned with a giant bottle of soda and glasses for everyone.

"You're flying in and out of the kitchen in eighty-mile-an-hour gusts," commented Mr. Sossi. But he took a glass of soda with everyone else.

Outside it got dark, and so Mrs. Sossi stood up and pulled down all the blinds. "Let's light some of the candles," she said. "I love candlelight."

"Won't that waste the candles?" asked Aldo.

"I bought plenty," she said, striking a match and lighting the candles on the table.

Peabody and Poughkeepsie walked about the room. Sometimes one of them stepped on the Monopoly board and knocked down some houses or a hotel. But they were set up again, and the game continued.

"The hurricane will probably come while we're asleep," said Mrs. Sossi.

"Hurricane Elaine is a slowpoke," said Aldo.

"I am not. I mean, it is not," said Elaine, defending her hurricane.

Finally it was bedtime. They put away all the parts of the Monopoly set. "This is so boring," said Elaine.

This time Aldo and Karen agreed with her. "That's the reason I stopped playing," said Karen. "It's a pain to put all the money away every time."

Aldo caressed a twenty-dollar bill. He wondered if he would touch a real one before the summer was over.

Mrs. Sossi blew out the candles, one by one. Everyone went upstairs to bed. "Don't be frightened if you hear the wind during the night," Mr. Sossi instructed his children. "This house is sturdy. A hurricane won't blow it down."

Aldo thought he would try to stay awake and listen for the storm, but he fell asleep and didn't wake till the next morning. The sun was shining, and the windows looked funny with all the tape stuck on them.

"Did I miss the storm?" he asked his mother.

"It was a false alarm," said Mrs. Sossi. "We don't have to worry about it after all." She showed Aldo the new headline in the newspaper: *Hurricane Elaine Fizzles Out at Sea.*

"How silly," said Aldo.

"How boring," said Elaine.

Muddy Sneakers

August's rainy weather canceled many of Aldo's swimming lessons. He was sorry because the better he became at this new sport, the more he liked it. But the rainy weather didn't bother him as much as it bothered his sisters. Both of them complained. Elaine had been perfecting her suntan. She said sun was good for her complexion and that it gave blond highlights to her hair.

Karen didn't worry so much about her appearance, but she said rainy days made her feel gloomy. She spent a lot of time writing letters to her pen pals. Aldo was always interested when she got a letter because he learned new things. He learned that it was winter in Africa while it was summer in Woodside, New Jersey. Yet even though Capetown, South Africa, was having winter, it was August there too. That was funny to think about.

Although he hadn't resumed his animals-on-wheels service, Aldo continued going with his mother to deliver the meals every Thursday. The stop at Mr. Puccini's was Aldo's favorite, but he found all the old people interesting.

One day Mrs. Thomas, who was the oldest person on their route, showed Aldo a patchwork quilt that she had. It had been made by her grandmother before the American Civil War. "Abraham Lincoln was just a young boy when my grandmother was sewing this," said

Mrs. Thomas. Of course, Aldo realized that Mrs. Thomas's grandmother didn't know Abraham Lincoln. Still, he felt as though he were touching history when he rubbed his fingers along the odd-shaped pieces in the quilt.

Aldo discovered that Mrs. Thomas would be ninety-three years old on her birthday. And her birthday was the same as Karen's, September first. Aldo tried to think what he could do to help make the day special when it came. He didn't know what you could give someone who was that old and didn't even have any teeth left. Furthermore, he had not been able to come up with any plan to acquire more money. He was feeling discouraged.

Mrs. Allenwood reported that the cast would be coming off her arm in another couple of weeks. "I'm from the school that says it's better to give than to receive," she told them. "When I'm better, I'm going to help deliver meals myself."

"Wonderful!" said Mrs. Sossi. "Perhaps you can help me and take over Aldo's job, since by then school will be open and I'll be minus an assistant."

When it wasn't actually pouring, Aldo spent a lot of time exploring his new neighborhood. With DeDe away, he didn't have a companion on his walks. Still it was interesting just to walk about. Aldo kept his eyes open and noticed things that other people might overlook. He saw earthworms that had crawled out of their wet holes and onto the sidewalk. He stopped many times to rescue worms that might otherwise be stepped upon by careless pedestrians. He picked up the worms and put them on nearby grass. When he lifted rocks, there were always slugs or crickets or other insects underneath. Usually they rushed to hide when Aldo uncovered their homes, but sometimes they stayed long enough for him to study them.

On one walk, Aldo discovered a squirrel

running down the street dragging a damp box of Cracker Jack. As Aldo watched, the animal stopped twice to rest before it reached a large maple tree. Then, clutching the box in its teeth, the squirrel climbed up the tree. When it was safe on a limb, it began eating the contents of the box. Aldo wondered if there were still a prize inside. "Chew carefully," he called up to the squirrel.

The Sossi garden looked worse and worse. Aldo had to restake the tomato plants because they were dragging on the ground. The plants needed a lot more sun.

When Aldo returned home from these excursions, his mother made him remove his sneakers and leave them outside. "They're too muddy," she complained. "I don't want that filth tracked into the house."

When Peabody and Poughkeepsie went outside on these damp days, they washed their feet as soon as they returned to the house. Both cats were very careful about keeping clean.

Aldo tried to imagine licking himself off to wash. Licking his fingers after eating ice cream would be all right, but he certainly wouldn't want to lick his muddy sneakers.

"It's a good thing that school will be starting in a few weeks," said Mrs. Sossi, looking at Aldo's feet. "I'll get you new sneakers for the new school year. The ones you have are a mess."

Aldo liked the idea of new sneakers, but he was not ready for school to open yet. He was enjoying vacation too much.

"Every week there is another expense," complained Mrs. Sossi. They had just been investigating pumps to put in their basement so that there wouldn't be floods in the future.

Talk like that made the ice-cream freezer seem more and more remote. Perhaps in a few years, when he was old enough to get a news-paper route, he could earn the money. Then he remembered what DeDe had said about inflation. Probably by the time he saved forty-nine dollars and ninety-five cents, the ice-cream freezer would cost one hundred dollars. It was very depressing.

Aldo missed DeDe. After she had been gone about a week, she sent Aldo a letter. It said:

Dear Aldo,
I caught eight frogs and I let them go.
I caught seventeen efts and I let them go.
I caught six fireflies and I let them go.
I caught one fish and I ate it.
Don't be mad.

Your friend,
DeDe

He knew DeDe wrote what she had because he was a vegetarian and didn't eat meat or fish. She didn't even know that Mr. Puccini had taught him so much about ichthyology. But of course Aldo wouldn't get mad at DeDe. You couldn't get mad at your best friend for eating supper, even if what they were eating were other friends of yours.

Then all at once Aldo's luck seemed to change. On the fifteenth of August, when there were only seventeen more days till Karen's birthday and twenty more days of school vacation, the sun came out. It shone so brightly that Aldo thought it wouldn't rain again for the rest of the month. At last he was able to go off to his swimming lesson. To his relief, he had not forgotten anything.

After a good lesson, Aldo went home. He was hoping there might be another letter from DeDe waiting for him. There wasn't, so he started looking through the *Pennysaver*, which had arrived that morning. He had given up looking for a job, but still he looked through the little newspaper out of habit. You never knew when you might find something interesting. Sure enough, midway through the pages, there was a large advertisement for the local shoe store. It read:

Grubby-Sneaker Contest
Any Woodside child up to age twelve can enter. Bring your worst-looking, most grubby, absolutely filthy and gross pair of sneakers at 10:30 A.M., August 31. The winner will be announced at noon that day and will be awarded a *free* pair of sneakers.

Aldo looked down at his feet. His sneakers were still caked with bits of dry mud. There was a small hole where he had torn the canvas when he fell off his bike one day. The sneakers were in bad shape, but they could be worse. Aldo decided that he would make them worse.

He showed the advertisement to his mother. "What a great way to save money!" said Mrs. Sossi, laughing. "I think you have a fair chance to win."

Aldo got an idea. "If I won the free pair of sneakers, would you add the money that you save by not having to pay for new sneakers to the ice-cream-freezer fund?"

So far there were only three dollars in his fund. (One dollar had come from two baby molars that had fallen out and for which he had collected fifty cents each.) Sneakers could cost as much as fifteen or even twenty dollars. The total amount would still be a lot less than he needed for the ice-cream freezer, but it was worth trying.

"Sure," agreed Mrs. Sossi. "I've nothing to lose."

Aldo could hardly wait to finish his lunch. He would have a busy afternoon ahead of him. He started thinking of the places in town where the sun wouldn't yet have dried up the puddles. He was determined that he would have the muddiest, grubbiest sneakers in the history of the world, or at least in the history of Woodside, New Jersey.

7

Hard Work

During the days that followed, Aldo kept his eyes on the ground. Wherever he walked, he was watching to see the effect upon his sneakers. He stepped everywhere and into everything: puddles, mudholes, and on rocks. He never stood still. He never sat still. He was busy wearing out his sneakers. At the same time, he was busy looking at other people's feet. He looked at the sneakers of the other boys and girls at the pool. He saw a pair of sandals that one of the girls was wearing. The straps were broken, and the sole was separating from the bottom of the shoe. Those sandals would have won first prize in an old-sandal contest, but Aldo didn't have to worry about them competing against him.

Another day Aldo saw two boys walking along on the main street of Woodside. One was wearing sneakers that looked much worse than Aldo's. He was a tall boy with red hair,

and his sneakers had once upon a time been red too. But now they were an indescribable color. The red-headed boy was walking with Michael Frank, who had been in Aldo's fourth-grade class.

"Hi, Michael," said Aldo.

"Hi, Applesauce," he responded, calling Aldo by his school nickname.

"Applesauce?" asked the red-headed boy.

"Yep!" said Aldo. "Who are you?"

"Trevor," he said. "I'm Mike's cousin."

"He's staying with me this week," Michael explained.

"When are you going home?" asked Aldo.

"Day after tomorrow probably," said Trevor.

"Oh," said Aldo. He almost said "good," but he caught himself in time. Trevor, with his worn-out sneakers, would be out of town before the grubby-sneaker contest.

"Well, see you around," said Aldo, hoping he wouldn't. The sooner Trevor left town, the better Aldo's chances of winning the contest would be.

Trevor's sneakers worried Aldo. He saw that his own were not as bad as they could be. So he started to work harder than ever. He hiked to the park, and he climbed on some jagged rocks there. Then he went home and offered to run any errands his mother might have. Next he walked over to Mr. Puccini's house, instead of taking his bike, even though he had been there the day before. Wearing out his sneakers was an exhausting business. Aldo wasn't sure he could keep up the same level of activity.

One night, when he was getting ready for bed and taking off his sneakers, Aldo thought what a shame it was that the sneakers wouldn't be getting any dirtier during the night. Too bad he couldn't invent some sort of robot that could walk about in his sneakers while he was sleeping. Then Aldo got an idea. He found a corner where nothing was growing in the garden and started to dig with his father's little spade. It wasn't easy to dig in the dark. He kept hitting hard things, which he knew were probably tree roots.

Mrs. Sossi called to him. "Aldo, what are you doing? Aren't you going to bed tonight?"

"I'll be right in," Aldo called back.

He kept digging until the hole was large enough to hold both of his sneakers. Then he covered them with the dirt and stones and walked barefoot into the house.

"How did you get so dirty at this hour?" asked Mrs. Sossi.

"Easy!" said Aldo, wiping the dirt from his hands onto his jeans. "My sneakers are camping out tonight."

"You'd better jump into the shower before you jump into bed," instructed his mother.

Aldo did so. As he stood in the shower with the water dripping down his back, he won-

dered if perhaps tomorrow night he should wear his sneakers into the shower. The water might add to the aging process. But he wondered how he could wear them into the shower and then bury them outside again.

Wearing out those sneakers was turning out to be hard work.

The Contest

DeDe returned from her grandparents' six days before the grubby sneakers were to be judged. "I wish I had known about it," she complained to Aldo, when he brought her up-to-date on the local news. She was wearing a pair of new purple sneakers that her grandparents had bought for her in Michigan. "My grandmother told me to throw my old ones away. She said they smelled."

"Not as bad as mine," said Aldo proudly.

He removed his left sneaker and held it up to DeDe's nose.

"Phew," she said, holding her nose. "If they judge by smell, you'll win for sure."

But on the day of the contest Aldo wasn't so sure. About twenty kids were gathered at the Walk Well Shoe Store, and each of them was carrying a pair of old, worn-out, dirty sneakers. Aldo stood wearing his good shoes and carrying his sneakers too. The shoes were practically new because he only wore them to church and on very special occasions. They had gotten too small over the summer, and they hurt his feet badly. His little toes were so squeezed that he could hardly walk.

DeDe had come along to watch the judging. "Yours look the worst," she assured Aldo.

He smiled at her. He was feeling nervous, and it was good to have someone around for moral support.

One of the salesmen handed out tags to each of the children. "Tie your sneakers together," he instructed them, "and then put your name and address on the tag."

None of the boys and girls had a pencil or a pen. The only time Aldo had even touched a pen all summer was when he had written his letter to DeDe. So the name writing took a long time as they all shared the two pencils provided by the store.

Finally all the sneakers were tied together and labeled and set in a long row. All the kids crowded around to look at them. They certainly made a dirty, muddy, smelly collection.

"Ouch." Someone stepped on Aldo's little toe. It hurt terribly, but he didn't care. If he won, it would be worth it.

"Come back at noon," said the salesman. "We'll have picked the winner by then."

The boys and girls started pushing their way out of the store. "Ouch." Someone stepped on Aldo's other toe.

"Do you want to go home, or what?" asked DeDe, when they got outside the store.

"I don't think I can walk anywhere," said Aldo. He sat down on the curb outside the store and removed his shoes. He massaged his little toes. "Let's just sit here," he said.

DeDe sat beside Aldo. He turned to face the shoe store. He wondered how the judging was going. Another girl was walking into the store with a pair of sneakers. He could see that they weren't nearly as worn as his. Now that his shoes were off and he could think about something other than his toes again, Aldo considered his chances of winning. He didn't think any of the sneakers looked as bad as his.

"I sure hope I win," he said to DeDe. "It's my last chance to earn some money this summer."

They saw two more boys coming down the street. The deadline for entering the contest was 10:30 A.M. These sneakers would probably be the last entries. The boys came closer. They were Michael Frank and his cousin Trevor.

"Hi, Frankfurter," DeDe called out.

Aldo didn't say anything. He was too surprised to see Trevor to remember anything else. Hadn't he said that he would be going home in a couple of days? Why was he still here? Trevor was carrying his old sneakers. Even after all the hard work he had put in, Aldo could see that Trevor's sneakers looked worse than his own. Now he would never win the contest.

"I thought you were going home," said Aldo. His voice sounded choked and strange as he spoke. He felt like crying.

"Yeah, I thought so too," said Trevor. "But my little sister just got chicken pox, and my aunt said I should stay on here so I wouldn't catch it from her."

The cousins went inside the shoe store.

Aldo felt awful. "Let's take a walk," he said to DeDe, as he started to put his shoes back on.

"I thought your feet hurt," she said.

"They're OK now," said Aldo. Even though she was his best friend, he didn't want to tell her that the disappointment of losing hurt even worse than his feet.

They walked slowly up the street, looking in the store windows. The stationery store had a big display of notebooks and pencils and other school supplies.

"Only four more days," said DeDe.

They walked on, stopping at each window. The ice-cream store had a sign about a new flavor that had been added to its list, *schoolberry*.

"What do you suppose that really is?" asked DeDe.

"It probably has pieces of homework chopped up inside it," said Aldo in a gloomy voice.

"Hey, don't sound so sad," said DeDe. "Even if school opens, we'll still have fun."

When they reached the hardware store, there was a big sign in that window too: *End-*

of-Summer-Sale! $10 Off the Price of Any Lawn Mower, Sprinkler Set, Plastic Pool, Ice-Cream Freezer.

For a moment Aldo felt great. "Hey look! The ice-cream freezer will only cost thirty-nine dollars and ninety-five cents now." But then he remembered that after paying back the borrowed quarters he had only three dollars saved. Now that he wasn't going to win the contest there was no way in the world he could earn thirty-six dollars and ninety-five cents by tomorrow, which was Karen's birthday.

"I guess Karen will have to wait until she's grown up to get the ice-cream freezer," Aldo said, sighing.

"She probably won't want it then," said DeDe. "Grown-ups never want the same things that kids do."

When they came to the bookstore, Aldo suggested that they go inside. "Maybe I can pick out a cookbook for Karen," he said.

Inside it was air-conditioned. DeDe found a cartoon book and sat down on the floor to look at it. Aldo went over to the cookbook section. He figured that he had enough money to buy two paperback cookbooks. The trouble was that there were so many books he didn't know how to pick just two. He began looking through them. "Are you planning to buy something, young man?" asked a salesman.

"I can't decide which is the best for my sister's birthday," said Aldo.

"That's a fine one in your hand," said the salesman. But there was something in his tone that made Aldo suspect he had never cooked a thing in his life. He probably didn't want kids hanging around inside his store.

"I think I'll ask my mother what she thinks I should buy," said Aldo, getting up.

"It's almost noon," said DeDe, when they were outside. "I can tell because I'm getting hungry." The clock in the jeweler's window agreed with DeDe's stomach. It was ten min-

106

utes to twelve. They walked back toward the shoe store. Aldo moved slowly, partly because his feet hurt in the too-small shoes and partly because he didn't want to see the sign announcing that Trevor was the winner.

A few boys and girls were already waiting in front of the store. They blocked the window so Aldo couldn't see the display of old sneakers. But he could read the big new sign that said, *If Your Child's Sneakers Look Like This It's Time for a New Pair.*

Aldo pushed through the crowd to look at the sneakers. He saw Trevor's old red sneakers right in front. He shouldn't have felt disappointed. He had known they would be there. But still he felt tears stinging in his eyes. He blinked quickly so that no one would see. As he stood at the window, the salesman brought Aldo's sneakers and placed them beside Trevor's. I guess I'm a runner-up, thought Aldo. They'll probably give me a pair of shoelaces!

The salesman held a sign that said First Prize, and he placed it next to Trevor's sneakers. He recognized Trevor in the group and said, "Come along, young man. I'll give you any sneaker in the store." Aldo watched as Trevor proudly went inside and sat down to be fitted.

DeDe watched Trevor too. Then she walked over to a contest poster. Aldo watched her reading it. He wondered why she was bothering now. Suddenly DeDe turned and grabbed Aldo. "Come with me," she said, pulling him into the store.

"It says on the sign that any kid who lives in Woodside can enter the contest."

"That's right," agreed the salesman. "But the contest is over now. The deadline for entering was ten thirty this morning."

"I know that," said DeDe. "But did you know that this boy doesn't live in Woodside?" She pointed her finger accusingly at Trevor. "So I don't think he can be the winner."

"What's your address?" the salesman asked Trevor.

"When I'm at home or when I'm visiting here in Woodside?" Trevor asked.

So that was how the first-prize sign was switched from Trevor's sneakers to Aldo's. Trevor was disqualified because he lived in Delaware, and visiting with his cousin in Woodside for two weeks didn't make him a resident.

Trevor's face turned as red as his hair. "I didn't mean to cheat," he said.

"That's OK," said the salesman, and to show that there were no hard feelings, he gave Trevor a pair of green shoelaces as a consolation prize. Every boy and girl who entered the contest got a pair of shoelaces too, but thanks to DeDe's quick thinking Aldo didn't get any. He got a brand-new pair of sneakers.

The last time Aldo had been shopping in the shoe store, he had selected a pair of blue suede sneakers. Mrs. Sossi quickly vetoed them because they were much too expensive.

Now Aldo could have any pair in the store for free. The salesman measured his foot. It had grown another half size during the summer, and the price of the blue suede sneakers had grown too. They cost three dollars more than they had in the spring.

The salesman put the new sneakers in their box and presented them to Aldo. DeDe stood nearby, smiling proudly.

"I can't wait to show them to my mother," said Aldo, when they finally left the store.

"I can't wait to eat," said DeDe. "It's way past lunchtime."

So Aldo and DeDe rushed back to Aldo's house, running most of the way, even though it was very hot and Aldo's shoes were still pinching his toes.

Ice-Cream-on-Wheels

Mrs. Sossi was speechless when Aldo showed her the prize sneakers. "And Mom, guess what! They reduced the price of the ice-cream freezer," said Aldo, without giving Mrs. Sossi even a second to make a guess. "Would you pay the difference plus the twenty dollars that these sneakers cost plus my three dollars? Then we'll have exactly enough to buy it today for Karen's birthday tomorrow," said Aldo breathlessly.

113

"I guess I will," agreed Mrs. Sossi, laughing. "Your father and I were talking about it again last night. Karen certainly wants it badly."

"Let's go right away before someone else buys it," said Aldo.

"What about lunch?" asked DeDe.

Mrs. Sossi told Aldo to sit down and catch his breath. After he and DeDe had something to eat, she would drive them into town to buy the ice-cream freezer.

"I'm too excited to be hungry," said Aldo.

"I'm excited, but I'm hungry too," said DeDe.

So they ate peanut-butter-and-strawberry-jam sandwiches. Aldo could eat only two sandwiches and drink only two glasses of milk because he was too excited to be hungry. DeDe ate three.

When they drove to the hardware store, Mrs. Sossi had trouble finding a parking space. To Aldo's disgust, she had to drive around

114

and around past the hardware store three times. The delay was more than Aldo could bear. Finally Mrs. Sossi found a space by a meter, but when she opened her purse, she discovered that she didn't have a dime. DeDe reached into her pocket for her emergency ten cents. It was two nickels, and they wouldn't fit into the slot.

"Here," said Mrs. Sossi, handing Aldo a quarter. "Run into one of the stores and ask for change. I'll wait in the car so we don't get a ticket. Otherwise, it will add another five dollars to the price of the ice-cream freezer."

Aldo had to go into not one, but three different stores before he could get change without making a purchase.

At last, however, he had a dime to put into the meter, and then the three of them could go to the hardware store.

"We would like to purchase the ice-cream freezer that you have on sale," said Mrs. Sossi.

Aldo stood beaming as the salesman took

it from the window. "You're in luck," he said. "This is the last one we have."

Mrs. Sossi paid him, and Aldo clutched the carton. Suppose someone had beaten them to it!

"I guess I really do have to call you Aldo Ice Cream now," said DeDe.

"I have never been so mortified in my whole life!" complained Elaine that evening, as the family was sitting around the dinner table.

"Mortification doesn't seem to have affected your appetite," said Mr. Sossi, as she reached for another piece of chicken. He had come home from his office later than usual this evening and so, although he had heard about Aldo's prize, didn't know yet about the ice-cream freezer hidden upstairs.

"What will people think?" asked Elaine. "It makes us look like slobs."

"No, it doesn't," said Karen reasonably. "It just looks as though Aldo is a slob." She looked at her brother, who was beginning his third ear of corn on the cob.

"I'm not a slob," said Aldo, swallowing the corn in his mouth. "I'm very neat for a boy my age. And I had to work very hard to win."

They were still talking about the grubby-sneaker contest. Aldo's sneakers were right smack in the center of the Walk Well Shoe Store window. And there was a big sign that said, *Bravo! First Prize Winner, Owner of the Worst-Looking Sneakers in Woodside, New Jersey: Aldo Sossi.*

"I've never won anything," said Karen mournfully.

"Well, I still think I'm going to change my name," said Elaine. "First that dud hurricane was named after me and now this. Elaine Sossi, sister of the grubby-sneaker winner. It's horrible."

"Guess what?" said Karen, brightening. "We were so busy talking about Aldo winning the contest that I forgot to tell you something very important. I walked past the hardware store today, and they had a sign in the window."

"Don't tell me that they also had a sign about Aldo's dirty feet," said Elaine, shuddering.

"My feet are clean. It's my sneakers that are dirty," Aldo protested.

"Not a sign about Aldo, silly," said Karen. "They had a sign about an end-of-summer sale. The ice-cream freezers are on sale!"

Aldo raised his corncob to cover his mouth and hide the smile he couldn't prevent. Wouldn't Karen be surprised when she received the ice-cream freezer that was hidden in his bedroom closet!

"Listen, Karen," said Mr. Sossi, "I don't want you to be disappointed tomorrow. I saw that sign, and I decided to splurge and buy you the ice-cream freezer. I stopped at the hardware store on my way home from work, and they told me that they had sold the last one this afternoon."

"Oh, then I won't get it for my birthday," said Karen sadly.

"Yes, you will," said Aldo, before he could stop himself. "Oh! I didn't mean to tell you. It was supposed to be a surprise for tomorrow."

"It *is* a surprise!" said Karen.

"It certainly is," said Mr. Sossi. "When did you get it, and how in the world did you pay for it?"

"This afternoon, with the sneaker money," said Aldo proudly, and he reminded his father about the arrangement he had made with his mother.

Karen insisted on seeing the machine at once, since it was only a few hours until her birthday. "Imagine if you had bought one, Dad," she said. "Then I would have two!" She began studying the directions and planning the flavors that she would make.

The Sossis gathered the supper dishes and put them in the sink. It was Elaine's and Karen's turn to wash up tonight. Aldo and his father had done the dishes the night before.

"Aldo," said Elaine, "how about working out some sort of money deal to buy us a dishwasher?"

"That's not a bad idea," agreed Mr. Sossi.

"He'd have to win the state lottery to be able to afford that," said Mrs. Sossi.

Aldo fed Peabody and Poughkeepsie their evening meal. Now that the contest was over and Karen's gift had been taken care of, he had just one more problem to solve. Tomorrow was Mrs. Thomas's birthday as well as Karen's. She was going to be ninety-three, which meant that she had been eighty years old the day that Karen was born. Aldo wanted very much to give her a present too, but he didn't have any money left at all.

Suddenly Aldo had an idea. He ran to his mother, who was sitting in the living room. "After we make our first batch of ice cream tomorrow, could we take some of it and deliver it to Mrs. Thomas? It will be her birthday as well as Karen's," he reminded her. As he spoke, the idea kept growing inside of him. "Maybe there'll be enough for all the people on our meals-on-wheels route. It would be a real treat for them if we could deliver some ice cream. I'm sure Karen would be willing to share with them."

"Bravo, Aldo," said Mrs. Sossi. "That's a lovely idea! It's much better than your cats-on-wheels. I know they would all enjoy it in this heat, and as no one is on a sugar-free diet on our list, they can all eat the ice cream."

Karen and Elaine finished washing the dishes and came into the living room. "Could we walk into town and buy the things we need for making our first batch of ice cream?" asked Karen.

"Can I come too?" asked Aldo. He didn't want to miss out on any part of this new venture.

"Sure," said Karen. "If it weren't for you there wouldn't be an ice-cream freezer here." She beamed happily at her brother.

Aldo looked down at his feet. "Wait a minute till I change out of these shoes." He had been so excited after the contest and buying the ice-cream freezer that he had forgotten how much the shoes had been pinching his toes all day long.

He ran upstairs to his bedroom and put on the new blue suede sneakers. They were the handsomest sneakers he had ever owned. Then he ran outside to catch up with Elaine and

Karen, who were waiting at the corner for him. He started to run through a puddle made by the lawn sprinkler of their next-door neighbor. Just in time he stopped himself. He certainly didn't want to get his prize sneakers dirty. He jumped over the puddle and ran on. Tomorrow he would show the sneakers off to Mr. Puccini and the others when he delivered the homemade ice cream. DeDe was right, he thought. Tomorrow he would really be Aldo Ice Cream.

He would miss helping with the meals once school started, but he knew he could still visit all his new friends in the afternoons. Aldo walked carefully around a second puddle. He had to keep his new sneakers very clean. School was starting in a couple of days, and he wanted them to look good. He had a feeling that it was going to be a good fall.

ABOUT THE AUTHOR

Born in New York City, Johanna Hurwitz received a B.A. at Queens College and an M.S. in Library Science from Columbia University. Formerly a children's librarian with the New York Public Library, Mrs. Hurwitz has worked in a variety of library positions in New York and Long Island. She lives in Great Neck, New York, with one husband, two children, and two cats.

Like Aldo and his family, Mrs. Hurwitz loves ice cream. Her favorite flavor is butter pecan.

ABOUT THE ILLUSTRATOR

John Wallner was born in St. Louis, Missouri, where he earned a B.F.A. in painting and graphics from Washington University. He also has an M.F.A. in graphics and art history from Pratt Institute in Brooklyn, New York. In addition to illustrating many award-winning children's books, Mr. Wallner has lectured and taught. His honors include exhibition in shows at the Corcoran School of Art in Washington, D.C., and the Society of Illustrators. In 1977, he received the Friends of American Writers Award for Best Juvenile Illustrator.

Mr. Wallner and his wife live in Woodstock, New York.